STARTERS ACTIVITIES

Growing things indoors

Macdonald Educational

About Starters Activities
These books cover a variety of activities for children at school or at home. The projects with their step-by-step illustrations, require the minimum of help from teachers or parents. Most of the words in the text will be in the reading vocabulary of the majority of young readers. Word and sentence length have also been carefully controlled. Extra information and more complex activities are included at the end of each book. Where possible, the child is free to invent and experiment on his own, but concise instructions are given wherever necessary. Teachers and experts have been consulted on the content and accuracy of these books.

Illustrated by: Robin Lawrie   **Managing Editor:** Su Swallow

Editor: Jennifer Vaughan   **Production:** Stephen Pawley, Rosemary Bishop

Special advisers: J. L. S. Keesing of the Royal Botanic Gardens, Kew. Gordon Message M.I.H.E. Headmaster of the Hamblett School, St Helens

Reading consultant: Donald Moyle, author of *The Teaching of Reading* and senior lecturer in education at Edge Hill College of Education

Chairman, teacher advisory panel: F. F. Blackwell, director of the primary extension programme, National Council for Educational Technology

Teacher panel: Loveday Harmer, Enid Wilkinson, Lynda Snowdon, Joy West

Colour reproduction by:
Colourcraftsmen Limited

© Macdonald and Company
(Publishers) Limited 1972

SBN 356 04033 X

Made and printed in Great Britain by:
Purnell & Sons Ltd, Paulton, Somerset

Filmsetting by:
Layton-Sun Limited

First published in 1972 by
Macdonald and Company
(Publishers) Limited
St Giles House
49-50 Poland Street
London W1

Contents

Miniature garden

This is a miniature garden.
You can make a garden
in a box.

Put stones in the bottom of the box.
Put soil on top.

2

Plant some seeds in the box.
Plant grass seeds and small flowers.
Give them a little water every day.
Soon they will start to grow.

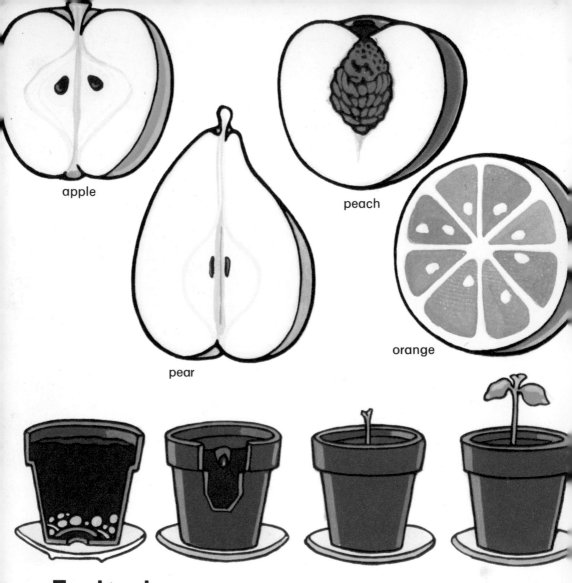

apple

peach

pear

orange

Fruit pips

Takes 2 to 3 weeks

Plant some pips in flower pots.
Keep the soil damp.
Small plants will begin to grow.

4

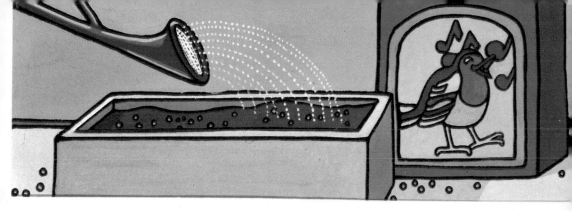

Bird seed

Takes 1 to 5 weeks

You can plant bird seed or hamster food.
Plant it in a box of soil.
Give it a little water every day.

5

Eggshell garden

Takes about 1 month

Fill some empty egg shells with soil.
Plant some candytuft seeds in them.
Do not let the soil get dry.

6

Soon the flowers will grow.
Try growing grass too.
Make a garden in an egg box.

Bulbs   **Takes 6 to 8 weeks**

You can grow bulbs in winter.

Plant them in soil.

Keep the soil damp.

8

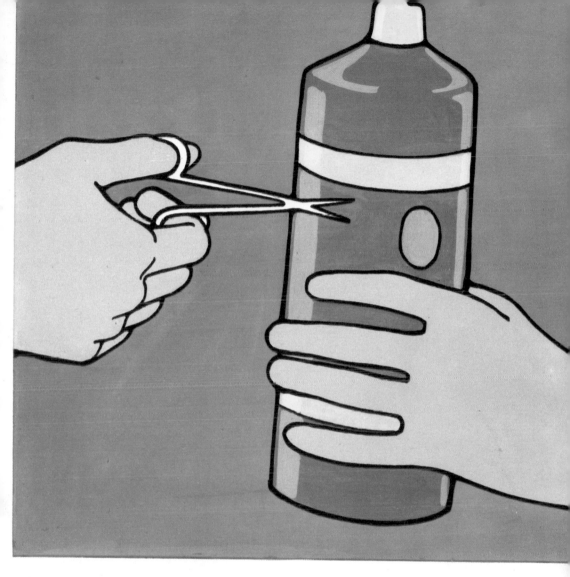

Crocus corms

Takes about 1 month

Cut the top off a plastic bottle.
Ask a grown-up
to cut holes in the side.

9

Fill the bottle with soil.
Push a crocus corm into each hole.
Put a corm near the top.

10

Plants grow upwards.
The crocus plants will grow
through the holes.
They will grow upwards.

11

Carnations

Takes 2 days

Here is a bunch of carnations.
You can make them all different colours.
Colour some water with ink.

12

Put the carnations in the water.
In a few days
they will change colour.

13

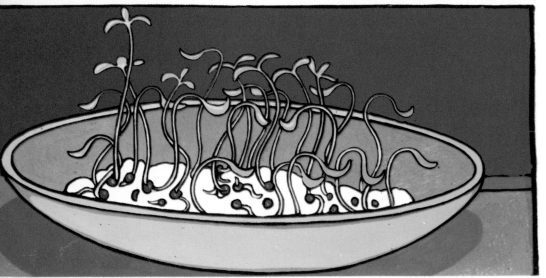

Cress

Takes about 5 days

Put some cotton wool in a saucer.
Put cress seeds on the cotton wool.
Keep them damp.

14

Soon the cress will grow.
It will have leaves.
After about a week
cut the cress with scissors.

Here are some cress sandwiches.
You can make a cress sandwich.
16

Potato

Takes 1 to 2 weeks

Try growing a potato in a box like this.
Keep the box closed.
The potato will grow
shoots, leaves and roots.

17

Orange faces

You can make faces like these
with oranges or grapefruit.
The hair is made of grass.

18

First cut the orange in half.
Scoop out all the fruit.
Fill the orange with damp soil.

Put the two halves of orange together.
Make holes in the top.
Plant grass seeds in the holes.
Stick a face on one half of the orange.

20

Pea

Most plants need light to grow well.
Put a pea on damp cotton wool.
Keep it by the window.
Try growing another pea in a dark place.

21

Growing Things words

miniature garden
(page 1)

orange
(page 4)

grass
(page 3)

peach
(page 4)

small flowers
(page 3)

candytuft
(page 6)

apple
(page 4)

eggshell
(page 6)

daffodil
(page 8)

ink
(page 12)

plastic
bottle
(page 9)

cress
(page 14)

crocus
(page 10)

potato
(page 17)

carnation
(page 12)

pea
(page 21)

23

Looking after plants

Plants die if they
have too much water.
Keep the soil damp,
but do not make it
into mud.

If a plant gets too big,
plant it in a new pot with
more soil.
Do not break the roots.

Most plants need light
to grow well.
Keep them by the window.

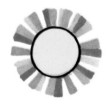

Make sure your plants
do not get too cold in
the winter. Do not
keep them too close to the window.

24

Some harder projects

A two-coloured carnation Slit the stem of a carnation down the middle, but not right up to the flower head. Do not bend the stem. Put half of the stem into a jar of red water, and the other half into a jar of blue water. Eventually you should have a carnation which is half red and half blue. This experiment illustrates the way in which water is drawn up by the stem and circulated to the flowers.

A two-coloured hyacinth Cut the bulbs of a blue and a pink hyacinth in half with a very sharp knife (this part of the experiment must be done by an adult). Take one half of each bulb and bind them tightly together with raffia. Plant this in a pot as you would any other hyacinth. When the plant flowers it should be a single hyacinth which is half blue and half pink.

Other seedlings Try growing seeds from trees in flower pots. Acorns will put up shoots which will soon look like little oak leaves. Try growing seeds from other trees, such as sycamore, horse chestnut, and sweet chestnuts. Potting compost is the best soil for any seedling. It is also good for bulbs (see pages 8 and 10).

Mustard and cress On pages 14, 15 and 16 we have described how to grow cress. Many people grow mustard and cress together. It is best to plant the mustard 2 days before the cress to be sure that both are ready at the same time.

Some harder projects

Pineapple plant

If you buy a pineapple find one with plenty of leaves on it. Cut the top off the pineapple about 3 centimetres below the leaves. Plant it in a pot with some potting compost, and cover all the fruit part. Keep the compost damp. Make sure the pineapple has plenty of light, and it will soon begin to grow. It is also possible to plant grape pips and date seeds, though date seeds take a very long time (5 or 6 weeks) to put up a shoot.

Cacti

You can buy cactus plants already potted, and some varieties produce colourful flowers. They do not need very much water, but if they are kept in a warm place they do need some. A miniature garden, or desert scene, for instance, can be made with sand and cacti.